One Hundred Days

With The Holy Spirit

Christopher Roberts

More Titles By Christopher Roberts

Can Be Found At The Link Below:

www.amazon.com/author/christopherroberts

About This Book

100 Days With The Holy Spirit is a daily devotional that you can use to gain an understanding about the work of the Holy Spirit throughout the entire bible. The Holy Spirit was there at the very beginning of creation, with the rest of the Godhead. The Holy Spirit has never been relegated from his position within the Godhead, contrary to the opinion of many who do not accept the workings of the Holy Spirit in some of our churches today.

We only need to read Genesis 1:1-3 to discover that when the earth was in darkness, the Holy Spirit hovered over the waters. With the involvement of the Holy Spirit in creation, God was able to utter those immortal words, "*Let there be light*" and the rest is history. From that moment onwards, the Holy Spirit has been fully engaged with God in the affairs of mankind.

Some Christians have not recognized that the Holy Spirit has been involved in both the Old Testament as well as the New Testament; including the Gospels. Different words are used to represent the Holy Spirit in the Old and New Testament. For example, in the Old Testament the term '*Spirit of the*

Lord is used to indicate that scripture is referring to the Holy Spirit. In the New Testament he is referred to as the *'Holy Spirit'* or *'Spirit.'*

In order to provide consistency, I have used the term *'Holy Spirit'* throughout the entirety of this book, whether I have used scriptures from the Old or New Testament. I have also split this book into two sections. In the first fifty chapters of this book we will consider the work of the Holy Spirit in the Old Testament. In the last fifty chapters of this book we will consider the work of the Holy Spirit in the Gospels and the New Testament.

I have limited each day's study to one page, so that you are not overwhelmed with endless notes before getting to the point. I have also provided a daily reading with each day's topic (I suggest that you only read one small chapter a day) so that you do not become overwhelmed with the material. There is no rush to get through this book; just spend 100 days to learn how the Holy Spirit can make a difference in your life.

I hope that this mini devotional will help you to recognize how important the Holy Spirit has been throughout the entirety of the bible. And if the Holy Spirit has been prevalent throughout scripture, the question is how important is the work of the Holy Spirit in our lives today? I hope that you will enjoy reading this book as much as I have enjoyed writing it.

Day 1

The Work Of The Holy Spirit

We start this book by considering the overall work of the Holy Spirit in the face of the earth. The Lord said in Genesis 6:3, '*My Spirit will not contend with humans forever.*' The Lord said this in the context of the fact that the earth was turning increasingly wicked, just before the flood came to devour the earth.

The overall purpose of the Holy Spirit is to convince people that they need Jesus, that they need to quit sin and that they need to obey God's word. Along with this mandate the Holy Spirit provides gifts, abilities and ministries to those who love him; to aid them in their efforts to pursued people that they need to turn to God through Jesus.

As we begin this journey with the Holy Spirit, we need to recognize that the operation of the Holy Spirit is still taking place throughout the earth. Those who suggest otherwise are short-sighted, with a limited understanding of the operation of the Holy Spirit in their lives. Today, God does not want you to be someone who is ignorant of the workings of the Holy Spirit throughout scripture.

Reading: Genesis Chapter 6

Day 2

The Gift Of Wisdom

It wasn't long before the gift of wisdom was displayed in the life of one of God's servants, in particular Joseph. In Genesis 41:38 it says, 'So Pharaoh asked them, "Can we find anyone like this man, one in who is the spirit of God?"' We know from Genesis Chapter 41 that Joseph had interpreted Pharaoh's dream, and that he had provided him with the necessary wisdom he needed to save Egypt from famine.

Can you imagine if Joseph had said, 'No I cannot provide Pharaoh with the wisdom he needs because I don't believe in the gifts of the Holy Spirit.' This may sound silly, but this is precisely what many Christians do today. And because they argue over the execution of the gifts of the Holy Spirit, they experience a spiritual famine akin to the natural famine Egypt would have suffered had Joseph not listened to the voice of the Holy Spirit.

Today, God wants you to listen to what the Holy Spirit is trying to say to the churches. He wants you to openly investigate the work of the Holy Spirit throughout the bible, and throughout church history. Without the Holy Spirit in your life, you will face a spiritual famine.

Reading: Genesis Chapter 41

Day 3

God Given Abilities

The work of the Holy Spirit is not just confined to the gifts of the Holy Spirit. Quite the contrary, many abilities that people have also come from the Holy Spirit. In Exodus 31:1-4 God filled Bezalel with wisdom, knowledge and skills in good, silver and bronze. This God did so that Bezalel would be able to produce the gold, silver and bronze works for the temple in the wilderness.

The problem we have in the West is that we distinguish too much between the physical realm and the spiritual realm. We somehow think that the spiritual realm belongs to God, and the physical realm belongs to us. But this is incorrect. Everything, both physical and spiritual, belongs to God. We think that such abilities like playing the keyboard, teaching students or developing skills in the workplace come from our own abilities in life.

Today, we need to recognize that God is all and in all. We need to acknowledge that everything we have, including our so called natural abilities, come directly from God who created us. So stop thinking that we have enabled ourselves to succeed in our chosen abilities and acknowledge that what we have has come directly from God.

Reading: Exodus Chapter 31

Day 4

Who's Leading You?

It did not take Moses long to recognize that he needed his elders to help him carry out the mission of leading Israel through the Wilderness. So God told Moses, in Numbers 11:16-17, to bring seventy of the elders to the tent of meeting to help him in the work. It was here that the Lord took some of the power of the Holy Spirit that was on Moses and put it on the elders.

Without the Holy Spirit these elders could not have helped Moses carry the burden, they would have collapsed with exhaustion by trying to serve God in the flesh. However, there are many people in our churches who are called to be in leadership, and have not got the necessary requirements to fulfill such a role. This is because they have not accepted the need to be filled with the Holy Spirit to get the work done.

If your church is being led by people who are not filled with the Holy Spirit, quite frankly you are going nowhere. You are being fooled by people who only know how to operate in the flesh. Today, ask yourself the question: *"Do I really want to be led by people who do not know the Holy Spirit?"*

Reading: Numbers Chapter 11

Day 5

~ Don't Turn To The Dark Side

One of the most shocking things that I have come across in Christendom is people who believe that the work of the Holy Spirit ended with the apostles, and yet they seek out spiritual things through other mediums. They read their horror scopes; turn to yoga for healing, along with dozens of other activities that belong to Satan.

God must be utterly insulted by such Christians who disagree with the gifts of the Holy Spirit, and yet turn to satanic things for help. God warned Israel, in Leviticus 19:31, not to turn to spiritualists and be defiled by them. Such Christians, who do not believe in the operation of the gifts of the Holy Spirit today, live in a vacuum.

However, here's the thing! There is no such thing as a vacuum. If we remove the work of the Holy Spirit from our lives and churches, that vacuum will be filled with something else. In other words, the devil will make certain that something belonging to him will fill the lives of these doubting Christians. Today, make sure that Satan is not the one who is whispering in your ears that there are no gifts of the Spirit available to you!

Reading: Leviticus Chapter 19

Day 6

Start Prophesying!

After the Holy Spirit had come upon the elders of Israel, as we observed on Day 4 of this book, two of the elders (Eldad and Medad) remained in the camp rather than going out to the tent of the meeting with everyone else (Numbers 11:26-29). However, the Holy Spirit came upon them and they prophesied in the camp.

Joshua petitioned Moses to stop these men from prophesying. Moses asked Joshua if he was jealous of these men prophesying. Moses then said that he wished all the Lord's people were prophets and that he would put his Spirit on all of them. Jealousy is often at the root of why some Christians resent other Christians prophesying.

According to Numbers 11:29, Moses believed that God wanted his Spirit on all of Israel and that all should prophecy. If Moses thought that this was important, then so should we. Do not let the jealousy in others prevent you from serving God through the use of the gifts of the Spirit. Jealousy comes from the flesh, and the flesh will always battle against the Spirit. So today, side with those of the Spirit and not with those of the flesh.

Reading: Numbers Chapter 11

9

Day 7

A Treasure In Human Vessels

There came a time in the history of Israel that Moses died. Thankfully, no vacuum was left after his death, and Joshua was able to step into the shoes of Moses and complete the mission to get the Children of Israel into the Promised Land. But in order that Joshua might lead the people into victory, he too needed to be filled with the Holy Spirit.

It says in Deuteronomy 34:9 that Joshua was filled with the spirit of wisdom, after Moses had laid hands on him. I cannot stress how important it is for us to lay hands on people and get them filled with the Holy Spirit. After salvation, this is one of the most important needs in a Christian's life. I have seen too many Christians lead defeated lives, all because they never allowed themselves to receive the Holy Spirit.

The Israelites listened and obeyed Joshua, not because of who he was, but because of the Holy Spirit within him. Today we need to come to the place of accepting who the Holy Spirit is, then we will discover a treasure in human vessels, and others will listen to us. So if your life lacks victory, it probably lacks the presence of the Holy Spirit.

Reading: Deuteronomy Chapter 34

Day 8

Spiritual Warfare

There was a period in history, between the period of Joshua and the monarchy, when King David reigned. This period of time was known as the Judges. During this period, Israel was in danger of losing the Promised Land due to not following the laws of God. God raised up various judges to deliver Israel from oppression. One such judge was Othniel, who was Caleb's younger brother (Judges 3:7-11).

During this time, the Spirit of the Lord came on Othniel so that he could become Israel's judge and go to war. And because the Spirit of the Lord was upon Othniel, he was able to overpower the king of Aram, thereby gaining peace in Israel for forty years, until he died. That is, God the Holy Spirit within Othniel enabled him to become a warrior on behalf of others.

Unless we are baptized in the Holy Spirit, we will never be able to conduct spiritual warfare on behalf of ourselves and other Christians. This is why the apostle Paul encourages us to put on the full armor of God in Ephesians 6:17. To conduct spiritual warfare, we need to be soundly saved and filled with the Spirit!

Reading: Judges Chapter 3

Day 9

Let God Change You!

In the Book of Samuel, we find that Israel was no longer happy with just having Samuel, or anyone to judge them. They wanted a king just like all the other nations around them. So God led Samuel to Saul, to make him king of Israel. But before Samuel anointed Saul as the new and first king over the nation of Israel, Saul needed an encounter with God the Holy Spirit.

In 1 Samuel 10:5-7, Samuel sent Saul to Gibeah to meet a procession of prophets, who were worshiping, playing musical instruments and prophesying. Remember, Saul had lost his father's donkeys, and was out looking for them at the time. Not only did Saul meet the prophets, the Holy Spirit came powerfully upon him, he prophesied and he became a different person (1 Samuel 10:10).

God's Holy Spirit is able to transform people's lives in incredible ways. Sadly, many Christians are stunted in their spiritual growth because they get saved, but then neglect the deeper work of the Holy Spirit in their lives; this leaves them spiritually impotent. Allow God's Holy Spirit to continue his work deep within your life today, and see what he will do for you!

Reading: 1 Samuel Chapter 10

Day 10

Have You Been Topped Up With Oil?

Sadly Saul did not remain obedient to God, and God rejected him as king in later life. This caused great sorrow for Samuel the prophet (1 Samuel 16:1-13). But God had a plan! God told Samuel to cheer up and go look for another king. So Samuel took his horn of oil and went to Jesse in Bethlehem to find the new king.

God told Samuel not to look on the outward appearance of people, but to look at the heart of a person. That is, judge people by their fruit and not just by what they say. Eventually, Samuel found David and anointed him with oil. In actual fact, if we search scriptures, we will find that David was anointed three times before he eventually became king. In other words, God is always willing to pour out more of his Holy Spirit on those who seek him.

From the day of David's first anointing the Holy Spirit came powerfully upon him, and the rest is history. Your future ministry happens due to three events: your birth, your salvation and your baptism in the Holy Spirit. If you have only experienced two of these events, then it's time to make sure that you have been topped up with oil!

Reading: 1 Samuel Chapter 16

Day 11

A Double Portion

Elisha recognized that everything Elijah did took place through the power of God the Holy Spirit. And because Elisha was going to replace the work of Elijah, he knew what he needed the Holy Spirit. This is why Elisha asked Elijah to let him have a double portion of his spirit, once he had been taken from him (2 Kings 2:9).

Elisha did not ask Elijah to provide him with the right contacts, or to teach him certain skills. Elisha went to the heart of the matter, and insisted that Elijah let him have twice the amount of power that he had availed himself of during his own ministry. If we count the number of miracles Elisha did during his ministry, he did fourteen miracles to Elijah's seven miracles.

It doesn't matter how many qualifications we have, or what skills we possess, without the work of the Holy Spirit in our lives those qualifications and skills will only take us so far in the kingdom of God. Yes God provides us with the skills that we need in life, but without his anointing on them they are limited. God is the same yesterday, today and forever, and if the saints of old needed the Holy Spirit, then how much more do we?

Reading: 2 Kings Chapter 2

Day 12

The Spirit of Encouragement

King David, like many people, went through some very dark days during his walk with the Lord. In 1 Chronicles Chapter 12, we discover that David was banished to Ziklag from the presence of Saul. At Ziklag he was joined by many of his warriors who supported him, including one particular warrior called Amasai in 1 Chronicles 12:18.

Here we discover that the Holy Spirit came on Amasai, who then declared to David that he would have success that those who helped him would have success and that God would help him. So David received these men and made them leaders of his raiding bands.

There are times when Christians are not always able to encourage themselves. At such times, God is able to anoint his servants to bring a message of encouragement to those who need it most. And should we discourage the moving of the Holy Spirit in people's lives, and then we restrict the encouragement God may want to bring to us through them. We can end up cutting off our spiritual noses to spite our religious faces if we are not too careful. Today let God use you to encourage others in Jesus name!

Reading: 1 Chronicles Chapter 12

ﾃ

Day 13

Plans Come From The Holy Spirit

When King David was planning to build the temple at Jerusalem, although it was Solomon who actually built it, he did not just come up with a good idea. It says in 1 Chronicles 28:12 that the Spirit put in his mind the plans for the entire project. In other words, David did not act on impulse; he acted on the powerful leading of God the Holy Spirit in his life.

We do not know how long David waited upon the Lord before the Holy Spirit gave him the plans for the temple. David may have had an idea in his heart that he wanted to see the building of the temple, but until those plans arrived he was going nowhere. David did not just come up with a good idea, hoping that God would bless his plans. No, David acted on the inclinations of the Spirit and not on his own ideas.

When we invite the Holy Spirit to take control of our lives, we will find that he will provide the blue print that we need to follow and have a successful Christian life. However, the opposite is true. If we don't invite the Holy Spirit to take control of our lives, we are in danger of heading towards disaster. Today, start asking the Holy Spirit to take control of your plans!

Reading: 1 Chronicles Chapter 28

Day 14

The Holy Spirit Will Bring You Peace

The period of the kings of Israel and Judah was a time when there were highs and lows, good kings and bad kings, etc. This was due to the fact that when Israel listened to God they had victory. When they disobeyed him they ended up in bondage. However, these kings needed to hear what God was saying to them through the power of the Holy Spirit.

In 2 Chronicles 15:1-2 the Holy Spirit of God came on Azariah, who went out to Asa king of Judah, and prophesied that the Lord was with him if he sought him, but God would forsake him if he forsook God. King Asa was obviously influenced by this short word through the prophet Azariah, because he brought great spiritual reforms to Judah. Asa took courage from this prophecy and removed the detestable idols from the land, and repaired the alter of the Lord (2 Chronicles 15:8).

Because Asa listened to the prophetic word, the land had no more war throughout his resign (2 Chronicles 25:19). Today, if you want to have peace throughout your Christian life, start to follow the leading of the Holy Spirit rather than trying to accomplish everything in your own strength.

Reading: 2 Chronicles Chapter 15

Day 15

The Battle Belongs To The Lord

In 2 Chronicles Chapter 20, the Moabites, Ammonites and the Meunites came to war against Jehoshaphat and Judah. Everyone from the towns of Judah came together with Jehoshaphat and sought the Lord for help. After they had petitioned the Lord, the Holy Spirit came on Jahaziel who brought the word of God to them.

Through the power of the Holy Spirit, Jahaziel prophesied that they were not to be afraid or discouraged because of the vast army that had come against them; the battle belonged to the Lord and not to them! As we read the rest of 2 Chronicles Chapter 20, we discover that Jehoshaphat and the rest of Judah only had to stand still and see the salvation of God at work on their behalf.

Because of the work of the Holy Spirit through Jahaziel, Jehoshaphat and the rest of Judah only had to worship God, while he took care of the enemy. So much so that Judah took three days to gather the plunder from the vast army that had come against them. If you want to take back what the enemy has stolen from you, then stand still and let God fight your battles!

Reading: 2 Chronicles Chapter 20

Day 16

The Spirit And The Word

After the captivity of Israel, God used Ezra to build the temple and Nehemiah to rebuild the city walls. Once the walls of the city were built, the Levites reminded Israel how often God had warned them by his Spirit, through the prophets. They told the Children of Israel that because they had not paid attention to the prophets, God had no choice other than to give them into the hands of their neighbors (Nehemiah 9:30).

This is a solemn warning in scripture; there are consequences for doing things through human flesh, and ignoring the leading of the Holy Spirit. And still various denominations argue over the use of the gifts of the Holy Spirit in churches today. The usual excuse for not believing in the gifts of the Holy Spirit is that because we have the bible, we don't need the gifts.

The Old Testament saints had the Pentateuch, which included the Law of Moses, and yet they still needed to hear the prophetic word delivered to them through the power of the Holy Spirit. And if the word and the Spirit were needed in the Old Testament, how much more are they needed in today's modern churches?

Reading: Nehemiah Chapter 9

Day 17

Who Left The Holy Spirit Behind?

Job went through the greatest trials a man could go through, other than Jesus when he suffered on the Cross. During his suffering, Job's comforters tried their best to encourage him, with little success. However, one of his comforters, Elihu, provided job with some much needed wisdom. Elihu told Job to recognize the importance of both God and the work of the Holy Spirit in his life.

This is why Elihu said that the Spirit of God had made him, and the breath of the Almighty had given him life (Job 33:4) As we have suggested before, many of the Old Testament people recognized that God was not alone in his dealings with mankind. And although scripture does not clearly state that there is a Trinity, we only have to read such statements as, 'The Lord Almighty', 'God' and the 'Spirit of the Lord' to recognize that God was three persons in one.

Today, I leave you with one question. If God was three persons under the old covenant, why do some people think that there are only two persons under the new covenant?

Reading: Job Chapter 33

Day 18

Take Not Your Holy Spirit From Me

When King David committed adultery with Bathsheba, the prophet Nathan came and warned him that God was going to deal with his sin. From this difficult time for David came the popular Psalm 51:10-12, 'Create in me a clean heart O God.' In one of the lines from this famous Psalm, David asked God not to take his Holy Spirit from him.

Of all the things that David could have been worried about at this time, the loss of the Holy Spirit in his life was preeminent. Nowhere in this Psalm does David fear that he might lose his salvation. In actual fact he prays, not that God would restore his salvation back to him, but that God would restore unto him the joy of his salvation. In other words, David wanted God to restore the joy of the salvation that he already had.

David's sin did not remove his salvation from him, only his fellowship and right standing with God. David was more concerned about losing the comfort of the Holy Spirit in his life, and so should we be. Today recognize that without the work of the Holy Spirit in our lives, we will never know victory, we will never know joy and we will never know peace.

Reading: Psalm Chapter 51

Day 19

Are You Spiritually Dry?

In Psalm 106, David provides a lengthy account of the rebellion that took place among the Israelites, during their forty year period in the Wilderness. David recounts events from leaving Egypt, the miracle of the parting of the Red Sea and Israel's time of complaining before God and Moses. Even Moses became more and more frustrated by their behavior.

By the time Israel had reached the waters of Meribah, the Lord was angry with them. Moses also got into trouble because of them, because he used rash words before God (Psalm 106:32-33). And the reason for all of this trouble was because Israel had in fact rebelled against the Spirit of God himself, which is why so many of them died before they reached the Promised Land.

Rebellion against the Holy Spirit, in these particular circumstances, was eventual physical death for many of the Israelites. Rebellion against the Holy Spirit today provides us with spiritual death. That is, we may not die physically when we rebel against the leading of the Holy Spirit, but way may in fact end up spiritually dry throughout the remainder of our journey with God.

Reading: Psalm Chapter 106

Day 20

Where Can I Go From Your Spirit?

Not only is God everywhere, so is his Holy Spirit. This is why David wrote in Psalm 139:7, '*Where can I go from your Spirit?*' Whether David went into heaven or into the depths, he could never escape the Holy Spirit. In fact, when we take a careful look at the life and words of King David, the Holy Spirit always had some kind of involvement with him.

Even like Samson, David knew the power of God in his life from an early age. This is why David was able to slay Goliath, in 1 Samuel Chapter 17, with one stone and while wearing no armor at the time. There is absolutely no limit for those children of God, who are prepared to accept the workings of the Holy Spirit in their lives every day.

The Holy Spirit should never be the occasional guest in our lives, and he should never be someone we refer to now and then. He should not be someone we hold theological debates about. The Holy Spirit should be an integral part of our everyday lives, speaking to us, leading us, energizing us and helping us to fulfill God's purpose in our walk with Him. Today, ask God to refresh you with more of the Holy Spirit in your everyday life!

Reading: Psalm Chapter 139

Day 21

Lead Me On Level Ground!

In Psalm 143:10, David asked God two things. The first was that God would teach David to do his will, and the second was that the Holy Spirit would lead him on level ground. In other words, David wanted to know God's will for his life. However, he also wanted God's will to be accomplished through the power of the Holy Spirit so that he might undertake God's will with no obstacles in his way. He wanted the path he walked upon to be smooth.

Knowing God's will and working out how to accomplish God's will in our lives are two different things. We may have understood God's will for our lives for many years, but we may not have really understood how to accomplish that will. We cannot accomplish God's will in our own strength. We need to allow the Holy Spirit to take control of our lives, and to lead us into God's destiny and purpose set out for us.

If you have been struggling to experience God's will being accomplished in your life today, then ask God to lead you into his will through the power of the Holy Spirit. No amount of self-effort will bring God's will to pass in your life. Submit to God and he will raise you up!

Reading: Psalm Chapter 143

Day 22

Experience God's Power For Yourself!

Before Jesus came to earth, Isaiah prophesied that God's Holy Spirit would rest on him giving him wisdom, understanding, counsel might, knowledge and the fear of the Lord (Isaiah 11:2). In other words, even Jesus could not, or would not accomplish God's will for his life without the involvement of the Holy Spirit. And if Jesus needed the Holy Spirit, how much more do we?

We should never take it for granted that such attributes as wisdom, understanding, counsel, might, knowledge and the fear of the Lord come through experience over the years. (Yes, some wisdom and understanding comes through experience) but God can also equip us with such attributes through the power of the Holy Spirit.

The level to which we put our trust in God's ability to provide us with certain attributes and gifts of the Holy Spirit will determine how much we operate in those gifts. (Today, don't keep turning to the flesh, other people or even books to find wisdom) Learn to experience God working through you by the power of his Holy Spirit!

Reading: Isaiah Chapter 11

W ed

Day 23

Learn To Consult God!

Isaiah prophesied that we should not become like obstinate children, who carry out plans that do not come from God, and always trust Egypt (the world) for their help (Isaiah 30:1-3). Yes we live in the world and we work in the world, but we should never put our trust in it. Sometimes it is only when people lose their jobs that they recognize the world is not as secure as they once thought.

Many people have felt ashamed because the security they thought their job had given them ended up nowhere. And the reason that people have felt ashamed is because they went down to Egypt without consulting God. In other words, God has no problem with us being involved in the world once we have consulted with him about what he wants us to do for him.

It may be that you have been hit hard through the recession, but that does not mean it is the end for you. As you consult God and allow him to reveal his plan for your life, you may find that God will allow you to pick up where you left off. Don't presume that because your world once came crashing down that God won't rebuild it again, because he will.

Reading: Isaiah Chapter 30

Day 24

Praying Women Part 1

In Isaiah Chapter 32, the prophet brought a special word to the women of Jerusalem. From that word the women of today can also take encouragement from the words of Isaiah. Isaiah warned the women that the fortress of Jerusalem would become abandoned, and the land would be wasted, but he did not just prophecy gloom and doom to them.

Isaiah told the woman that this gloom and doom would last until God poured out his Holy Spirit upon them from on high. Then the dry desert would become a fertile field, and the fertile field would become like a forest (Isaiah 32:15). All my life I have heard how God has poured out his Holy Spirit due to the efforts of praying women. In other words, no matter how bad the recession may have been for us, women who pray make a difference.

Today is not a day when we should think that the desert will always remain dry for us. Today is the day when we need to ask God to pour out his rivers of living water on the land, so that the desert might become fertile once again. Has God placed a burden upon your heart concerning the state of your nation? Then start praying until it begins to rain again!

Reading: Isaiah Chapter 32

Day 25

Praying Women Part 2

Isaiah not only prophesied about the state of Israel and her rebellion against the Lord, but he also spoke about judgment coming upon all the nations (Isaiah Chapter 34). God is a God of love, but that does not mean that he is a pushover. It does not take a genius to recognize that judgment is coming upon the nations today, particularly relating to finances, the climate and the economy.

The reason why that judgment might be coming upon the nations is because money has become more important than God for many people, including Christians. In Isaiah 34:16-17, the prophet said that we should look to the scroll (God's Word) and read the encouragement found therein. He stated that none of these would be missing, and not one will lack her mate. This is because God had given the order, and his Holy Spirit will gather them together.

Woman of God, the Lord has not finished with you just yet. As you put God first and continue to seek his face, then he will provide for you. He will bring you together with those who are like minded, and you will not fail.

Reading: Isaiah Chapter 34

Day 26

Take A Leap Of Faith

In Isaiah Chapter 40 we find the prophet comforting God's people, but we also find him asking them a question. The prophet asked them, in Isaiah 40:13, "*Who can understand the Holy Spirit, or instruct the Lord as his counselor?*" In other words, not only can we not instruct the Lord, but we cannot understand the Holy Spirit from a natural perspective. That is, the Holy Spirit is not naturally discerned.

The Holy Spirit operates through faith, and not by trying to figure him out. We can sit and debate with people about the need for the Holy Spirit until the cows some home, but such debates usually lead us nowhere. It's time to stop debating with other people about the merits of the Holy Spirit, and start seeking God for yourself.

I would rather be influenced by the Holy Spirit than be influenced by other people, who may be operating in the flesh. But until we have partaken of the baptism in the Holy Spirit, we will not really understand how he operates in our lives. Remember, God the Father, God the Son and God the Holy Spirit are all above the counsel and understanding of people.

Reading: Isaiah Chapter 40

Day 27

Don't Put The Cart Before The Horse!

There's a saying, *'Never put the cart before the horse.'* There are too many Christians who think that they are serving the purpose of God in their generation. Sadly, many of them have been led astray by the plans of others, plans that do not originate in heaven. In other words, they step out in presumption, hoping that God will bless their endeavors.

I've got news for you; God will not bless your plans if they are not his plans, no matter how hard you work for the kingdom of God. As we discussed earlier, Jesus was equipped by the Holy Spirit before he went about his Father's business. In Isaiah 42:1, the prophet said that God would put his Holy Spirit on Jesus, and then he would bring justice to the nations.

You may have many ideas and plans about how you want to serve the Lord, which is not a bad thing. However, what you need to discover is which of those plans come from God, and which come from you. Today, begin to ask God to lead you by his Holy Spirit into the plans that he has for you. And be prepared to let go of those plans which do not have God's approval on them.

Reading: Isaiah Chapter 42

Day 28

God's Blessings Belong To You

The biggest mistake that some Christians make is to presume that the blessings found in the Old Testament belong only to the Children of Abraham; that is, the Jews. This is not the case! Every blessing we find in the bible, whether they are in the Old Testament or in the New Testament can be appropriated by Christians.

When I was going through a difficult time once, I began to search out God's blessings in the bible, particularly in the Old Testament. I began to pray over these blessings and soon my faith began to rise within me, until God gave me the victory over my circumstances. In Isaiah 44:3 God promises to pour water on the thirsty land, and the Holy Spirit on your offspring.

In other words, God's blessings are not just for a moment in time, they are for a life time and into eternity. God's blessings and God's Holy Spirit are not limited just to Israel; they are available to the whosoever. Today tell God that you are thirsty, and tell him you believe that every single one of his promises belong to you. Learn to highlight God's promises throughout the bible, and start to believe that they will come to pass in your life.

Reading: Isaiah Chapter 44

Day 29

The Holy Spirit And The Word Are One

Learning to trust the work of the Holy Spirit in our lives gets easier the more that we let go of our own plans. We must never forget that the outpouring of the Holy Spirit on our lives relate to a covenant God made with his people in Isaiah Chapter 59. That covenant was not a momentary covenant, as we alluded to in the last chapter of this book. It is an eternal covenant, which applies to those who will seek after God with all their hearts.

In Isaiah 59:21, the covenant God has made with us states that the Holy Spirit within us will never depart from us. Not only so, but they who have the Holy Spirit have God's word in their mouths, which will always be on their lips. The simple fact is that the Holy Spirit and the word, through the bible, are one. Neither the Holy Spirit nor the bible contradicts each other, and those who suggest otherwise are only trying to deceive you.

Today, God wants you to be in tune with both the bible and with God the Holy Spirit. He does not want you to only have half an experience in the things of God. So do not be put off by those who are, quite frankly, non-believers. Enjoy both God's word and the Holy Spirit on a daily basis!

Reading: Isaiah Chapter 59

Sua

Day 30

Do You Want A Spirit-led Ministry?

Your ministry must be Spirit-led if you are to become fruitful in the things of God. I do not care how important or influential a church leader thinks s/he is, if they are not anointed by God the Holy Spirit to minister to others, then they are going nowhere as far as God is concerned. Too many people are still influence by those who suggest that they can serve God through their own efforts, rather than through being led by the Holy Spirit.

Listen to what it says in Isaiah 61:1 NIV, 'The Spirit of the Sovereign Lord is on me, because the Lord has anointed me to proclaim good news to the poor. He has sent me to bind up the brokenhearted, to proclaim freedom for the captives and release from darkness for the prisoners.' Not only did this scripture apply to Jesus, it applies to us too.

Today if you will seek for more of God's Holy Spirit, as Elisha did (and as we discussed earlier in this book), then God will anoint you to preach the good news, bind up the broken hearted, proclaim freedom to those in captivity and release those who are imprisoned in darkness. Then you will discover how fruitful you will become!

Reading: Isaiah Chapter 61

Day 31

Don't Run Dry!

Because the Holy Spirit never speaks of himself, his influence is not always obvious when we read the Old Testament. Isaiah takes us back to the days when Moses led Israel out of Egypt and through the Red Sea (Isaiah 63:11). Not only did God part the waters for Israel to travel through on dry ground, but God also set the Holy Spirit among them, even though this was not originally highlighted in the Book of Exodus.

The reason that the Holy Spirit was present among the people was because God had set him there to begin with. Today, people think that they can separate God the Father, God the Son and God the Holy Spirit from each other, but this is error. The three members of the Trinity work together; for us to separate them out, suggesting that the Holy Spirit has no involvement with us in these last days of time, is bad theology.

Remember, it was not always obvious to the Israelites that Jesus was with them in the Wilderness, but we know that he was the Rock who provided the water that they needed every day. Today, do not try and separate the Holy Spirit out from the rest of the Trinity, otherwise you will run dry.

Reading: Isaiah 63:1-13

Day 32

Let The Holy Spirit Reveal God's Word To You

When we begin to recognize that the Holy Spirit has always had an involvement in everything that God has done in the face of the earth, then we will enter a rest that we did not think possible. Isaiah said that Israel were like cattle who were given rest by the Holy Spirit (Isaiah 63:14). In fact, Isaiah goes on to state that the Holy Spirit was the key that God used to guide his people with.

There are many keys to God's kingdom, which we will discover when we allow the Holy Spirit to reveal scripture to us. I have met many preachers who only know how to use commentaries to reveal the meaning of scripture, as they prepare their sermons. Such commentaries should never replace the leading of the Holy Spirit when it comes to interpreting God's word.

I have discovered more revelations through scripture when I have let God's Holy Spirit reveal the hidden manner therein. Today, you don't just need a commentary to find out what God wants to reveal to you in scripture, you need the presence of the Holy Spirit. So, ask God to reveal his word to you through the power of the Holy Spirit.

Reading: Isaiah 63:14-19

Day 33

Make Yourself Vulnerable To God!

When God wanted to speak to Ezekiel, in Ezekiel 2:1-2, the Holy Spirit came into him and raised him to his feet; then Ezekiel heard God speaking to him. The reason why people attempt to dismiss the Holy Spirit and his gifts today is because they are actually afraid of the Holy Spirit coming into them. And we can appreciate that some people will feel vulnerable when they ask the Holy Spirit to enter them.

But that's the key to receiving the Holy Spirit, being vulnerable before God and opening ourselves up to him. Ezekiel had no problem in doing this and neither should we. And because Ezekiel allowed the Holy Spirit to come into him, he was able to hear God speaking to him. And this is one of the keys to God's kingdom.

Today, if you want to hear God more clearly, start to open yourself up to God; become vulnerable and invite the Holy Spirit to come right inside of you. You have nothing to fear by letting the Holy Spirit enter you. He will not harm you in any way. Too many Christians miss out on what God wants to say to them; don't let yourself be one of them!

Reading: Ezekiel Chapter 2

Day 34

Don't Let People Limit You!

Ezekiel recounts an experience where the Holy Spirit lifted him up and he experienced the glory of the Lord (Ezekiel 3:12). Not only so, but he had a further experience where the Holy Spirit lifted him up and took him away to visit the exiles who were living in Tel Aviv (Ezekiel 3:14-15). I have heard of many people who have literally been moved around the planet by the power of the Holy Spirit.

There are no limitations to the kingdom of God and there are no limitations to what the Holy Spirit can do in our lives as we submit to him. The only limitations on the Holy Spirit, the power of God, are the limitations that we put on him. Those limitations are in our minds, which are like chains that would try to bind us. But God does not run his kingdom based on the limitations we would place upon him.

Are you tired of the limitations people would try and put on you? God the Father and God the Holy Spirit have no limitations on them. If you are a person who has not reached your full potential because people have tried to limit you, today you need to break free in Jesus name!

Reading: Ezekiel Chapter 3

Day 35

Bring Your Vessel!

The Holy Spirit is the power of God upon the earth. He convinces and convicts us of sin, and shines his light on those areas of our lives which are not pleasing to God. But when we ignore God's warnings to us, through the power of the Holy Spirit, then we will end up in bondage.

Ezekiel was lifted up by the power of the Holy Spirit, where in visions God took him to Jerusalem to see the idolatry and detestable things that the elders of Israel had been up to in darkness (Ezekiel 8:8,12). The reason that many people do not want to accept the Holy Spirit into their lives is because they want to lead a double life. They want to be seen as people who attend church, yet they lead unclean lives in the privacy of their own homes. They think that God the Holy Spirit won't see such detestable things.

If you are a person who has struggled to serve God because the bondage of sin won't let go of you, or you won't let go of sin, and then ask God to fill your vessel with more oil. Sin is dealt with through the blood of Jesus and the power of the Holy Spirit to release you from bondage. So bring your vessel to God today, he wants to give you more of the Holy Spirit.

Reading: Ezekiel Chapter 8

Day 36

Don't Travel Alone!

As we have discussed before in this book, when we ask God for the Holy Spirit, we do not need to worry that God will give us something, or someone who would do us harm. In fact, those who are filled with the Holy Spirit have a keen desire to serve the Lord, simply because God's desire suddenly becomes their desire.

At the beginning of Ezekiel 11:1, the Holy Spirit lifted Ezekiel up and brought him to the gate of the house of the Lord. In other words, the Holy Spirit will enhance our spiritual experience and not detract from it. In fact, it is hard to understand how Christians without the Holy Spirit can motivate themselves to serve God, or even attend church without becoming religious.

If you have been trying to motivate yourself to serve God or motivate yourself to go to church, then maybe you need to ask God to either baptize you with the Holy Spirit or ask God for more of the Holy Spirit. What you don't want to do is end up where you have to force yourself, through your own efforts, to serve God. The journey God has placed us on is a long one, so do not travel that journey alone.

Reading: Ezekiel Chapter 11

Day 37

Let The Holy Spirit Bring You Into Victory

Christians who find it hard to obey God's commands are often people who have tried to obey such commands through self-effort in the flesh. God said to Ezekiel that he would put his Holy Spirit in him and move him to follow His decrees; so that he would be careful to follow God's laws (Ezekiel 36:27). In other words, God's Spirit within Ezekiel was the one that would enable him to keep God's commandments by the Holy Spirit.

We have all come across Christians who struggle to follow God, and who struggle to keep away from the things of the flesh. In fact, you may very well be a person who wants to do what is right, but temptations overtake you. Remember, after Jesus was baptized and after the Holy Spirit descended on him, that's when he went into the Wilderness to be tempted of the devil.

Christians should never try to overcome temptations through self-effort. We should allow the Holy Spirit to put to death the deeds of the flesh. Fighting flesh with flesh will get us nowhere. However, when we trust God to put to death the deeds of the flesh through the power of the Holy Spirit, then we will have victory.

Reading: Ezekiel Chapter 36

Day 38

Get Out Of The Valley Of Dry Bones!

Have you ever felt as if you were in a deep valley that was full of dry bones? It says in Ezekiel 37:1 that the hand of the Lord was on Ezekiel, who brought him out by the Holy Spirit to a valley of dry bones. Throughout the rest of Ezekiel Chapter 37 God commanded Ezekiel to prophecy into the valley of dry bones so that they might live, and so that a vast army would come to life.

After Ezekiel had prophesied to these dry bones, God told him that this was the house of Israel, who's hope were dry and who's bones were gone (Ezekiel 37:11). That is, God would put his Holy Spirit into the house of Israel, who were in captivity, and bring them back to their own land (Ezekiel 37:14). In other words, by the power of the Holy Spirit, Ezekiel was able to follow God and bring hope to Israel, who was in bondage in Babylon.

Today, God wants to use you to speak through the power of the Holy Spirit and bring hope to those who are in bondage. People may not normally listen to what you have to say. However, they will listen when you are anointed by God to bring the word of prophecy to those in need.

Reading: Ezekiel Chapter 37

Day 39

Going Deeper With God Part 1

The outpouring of the Holy Spirit is not for just a chosen few, but the Holy Spirit is for everybody who will come to the Lord. God will even pour out his Holy Spirit on unbelievers in an effort to bring them to repentance. Originally the Holy Spirit was for the whole house of Israel, according to Ezekiel 39:29. But today, God wants to pour out his Holy Spirit on all flesh.

When God said to Ezekiel that he wanted to pour out his Holy Spirit on the house of Israel, this was because God did not want to hide his face from them any longer. The outpouring of the Holy Spirit gives us a fresh revelation of who God is, because he is no longer hidden from us. We do not need to see God's face to recognize who he is, although we have seen God through the face of Jesus.

The Holy Spirit can reveal to us the very essence of God in a way that no other can reveal him to us, although we know God through the life of Jesus, as stated above. Today, if you feel that you need to experience the very essence and presence of God deep within you, ask the Holy Spirit to help you gain a greater revelation of who God is!

Reading: Ezekiel Chapter 39

Day 40

Going Deeper With God Part 2

Ezekiel had an experience where the Holy Spirit lifted him up and brought him into the inner court of the temple. Here Ezekiel experienced the glory of the Lord in a powerful way (Ezekiel 43:5). Salvation brings us to God through the work of Jesus on the Cross, where he died to take our sins away. We were granted access to the Father through the Son, which is the gospel message.

However, many Christians feel that they want to go deeper with God, and experience him more intimately, even after salvation. Some Christians feel that they are lacking in one way or another. Jesus brings us to God and the Holy Spirit brings us deeper into the center of God's being, as we intimated in the last chapter of this book.

Yes salvation is a completed work, but that does not mean we cannot go deeper into God. People get these two concepts mixed up. They think that salvation is the only thing that God has to offer us. Yes salvation is the most important work, but God's work in our lives does not end at salvation, it's just the beginning; so don't forget that!

Reading: Ezekiel Chapter 43

Day 41

World Leaders Need God - Part 1

Although there is no direct mention of the Holy Spirit in the Book of Daniel, Nebuchadnezzar acknowledged that the spirit of the holy gods was in the prophet and that he was able to interpret dreams (Daniel 4:9). Even though Nebuchadnezzar did not acknowledge the Holy Spirit directly, we know from reading this passage of scripture that he was in fact referring to the work of God, through the Holy Spirit, in the life of Daniel.

We know from the rest of Daniel Chapter 4 that Daniel was able to warn Nebuchadnezzar that his majesty would be brought low, for not acknowledging that God had raised him up. Nebuchadnezzar had claimed that he had raised himself up instead of God doing it.

Today I am of the opinion that we need to see genuine powerful prophets raised up; those who walk close to God and who can bring the word of God into the lives of world leaders. Nebuchadnezzar was one of the most powerful leaders in history, and yet he was prepared to hear the word of the Lord. Today pray that world leaders will take heed of their circumstances, and that they will seek God to help them govern their nations.

Reading: Daniel Chapter 4

Day 42

World Leaders Need God - Part 2

Daniel had many encounters with the rulers of Babylon throughout his entire lifetime. This included an incident when King Belshazzar held a banquet for a thousand of his nobles, where they all drank wine from the silver goblets which belonged to God's holy temple in Jerusalem (Daniel 5:2). It wasn't long before the writing was on the wall for Belshazzar, which left him with his knees knocking in fear (Daniel 5:6).

Again, Daniel's reputation had gone before him as a man full of the Holy Spirit. Daniel was brought before Belshazzar, so that he could interpret the writing on the wall. Belshazzar acknowledged he had heard that the spirit of the gods was in Daniel (Holy Spirit) and that he had insight, intelligence and understanding in wisdom.

Today's world leaders neither recognize nor acknowledge that Christians have the answer to their problems, because the spirit of the holy gods is in them. If our world leaders will not listen to us and acknowledge God in their lives, then we need to pray that God will move on them, and guide them away from the path of destruction they are heading along.

Reading: Daniel Chapter 5

Day 43

Day Of The Lord - Part 1

God is no respecter of persons and neither is the Holy Spirit. God said, through Joel the prophet, that in the last days he would pour out his Holy Spirit on all flesh. Such an outpouring would enable sons and daughters to prophecy, with old men having dreams and young men seeing visions (Joel 2:28). It is noticeable that there is no distinction over who can prophecy, which included men and women, young and old alike.

We are now living in the time frame of the last days, when Joel's prophecy would be fulfilled. And part of God's word to us is that the outpouring of the Holy Spirit would include the ability for men and women to prophecy, which is why the apostle Paul said that we should not forbid prophecy. Prophecy is one of the hallmarks of the end times, which is why the enemy delights in bringing false prophets onto the scene.

Today, do not be put off because of the many false prophecies taking place in the world, that's just the enemy trying to copy what God is trying to accomplish in our lives. Allow God to use you in prophecy, and you will be fulfilling God's word through Joel the prophet!

Reading: Joel 2:1-28

Day 44

Day Of The Lord - Part 2

Not only does God want to do great things through the life of his servants, he wants to show wonders in the heavens and on the earth (Joel 2:29-30). The events forecasted in the remaining verses of Joel Chapter 2 indicate that external changes will start to take place, up to the coming of the Lord Jesus Christ.

Towards the very end of these last days of time, the sun will be darkened and the moon will turn to blood just before Jesus returns. But this does not mean that God will not be working in the lives of people in these last days of time. It says in Joel 2:32 that during this period, everyone who calls on the name of the Lord will be saved. This also means that there will be deliverance on Mount Zion and in Jerusalem.

Do not let anyone prevent you from continuing to serve the Lord in these last days of time. Until and unless God tells you to stop, there is still work to be done in God's kingdom, no matter how dark the world becomes. God's Holy Spirit within you is greater than anything in the world; so do not fear what is happening around you, only fear God!

Reading: Joel 2:29-32

Day 45

You Are A Child Of The King?

Although the prophet Micah came after the book of Daniel and other books in the bible, he actually performed his ministry in the reigns of Jotham, Ahaz and Hezekiah, who were the kings of Judah, and before Israel was exiled to Babylon. Although Micah was a prophet of doom, he also brought prophecies of hope to those who would hear what he had to say to them.

What was interesting about the prophet Micah was that he knew who he was in God, and he knew that God the Holy Spirit was working in his life. In Micah 3:8 the prophet said of himself that he was filled with power, with the Holy Spirit, etc., and he would declare Israel's sin to them. In other words, Micah was not full of himself; he knew that God the Holy Spirit resided within him, and gave him the power to do what God had commanded him to do.

God expects no less of us. He expects us to acknowledge that God the Holy Spirit is within us, and that he has given us power to serve him according to his will. Today stop seeing yourself as a failure, someone who Satan has tried to put down. Rise up in the name of Jesus, and recognize that you are a child of the King!

Reading: Micah Chapter 3

Day 46

Do Not Fear - Part 1

Although the Holy Spirit is not mentioned in Haggai Chapter 1, it is clear that God was at work among those who had returned from captivity and back to Jerusalem. In Haggai 1:13-14, the prophet told the returnees that the Lord was with them. At that point the Lord stirred up the spirit of the governor of Judah, the high priest, and the whole remnant of the people.

Because God had stirred them up through the Holy Spirit, they were able to get to work on the house of the Lord. It did not matter what God's house looked like, everyone got on board and helped with the rebuilding program. As we know from both the Book of Ezra and the Book of Nehemiah, the temple and the temple wall at Jerusalem were rebuilt to the satisfaction of all concerned.

It is easy to become fearful when we recognize how much work needs to be done in the kingdom of God today. We know that there is plenty of work to be done, with few people available to serve God. We need to ask God to stir up his people to start serving him in these last days of time, just like Haggai was used by God to stir the remnant into service in his day.

Reading: Haggai Chapter 1

Day 47

Do Not Fear - Part 2

Just like the children of Israel, many Christians find themselves going through a wilderness experience. However, when they come out of their wilderness experience, things do not always appear as they were before they went in. In Haggai 2:3 the prophet asked, "*Who saw the house of God in its former glory and what does it look like now? Does it look like nothing?*"

Although the children of Israel were disappointed when they looked at the state of the house of God as it was then, Haggai told them not to be discouraged. In Haggai 2:4 the prophet told the people to be strong because God was still with them. And this was despite what the house of God currently looked like. In Haggai 2:5 the prophet also told Israel that God's Spirit was still with them, and that they should not fear.

Today do not become fearful, even if you think that the church is not what it was like twenty years ago or so! It does not matter what the church looks like now, it's whether or not God's Holy Spirit is still active in the world that counts. Don't look to the building! Don't look to other Christians! Look to God who still supplies his Holy Spirit, and do not fear!

Reading: Haggai Chapter 2

Day 48

It's Not By Might

God sent Zechariah to encourage those who were involved with the rebuilding of the temple, at a time when they were feeling discouraged after they had returned from Babylon and back to Jerusalem. Zechariah had a vast number of visions and prophecies for those who were rebuilding the temple at Jerusalem, which are well documented in the Book of Zechariah.

Among those returning to Jerusalem from Babylon was a man named Zerubbabel, who was one of the leaders. During one of Zechariah's vision, he received a specific word for Zerubbabel in Zechariah 4:6, "*It's not by might, it's not by power, but it's by my Spirit says the Lord.*" In other words, Zerubbabel did not need the might of an army, or the vast resources of an empire to complete the major work of rebuilding God's temple at Jerusalem. All he needed was God the Holy Spirit to work through him and get the job done.

You do not need the vast resources of some of the major ministries you have seen on Christian TV to get the job done. All you need is God the Holy Spirit to help you complete the work that he has anointed you to do.

Reading: Zechariah Chapter 4

Day 49

Are You Ready?

God gave Zechariah a tremendous vision of four chariots, which represented four spirits which came out from standing in the presence of the Lord (Zechariah 6:1-5). The role of these spirits was to bring rest to the four corners of the world; or the nations around Israel. We know that before the captivity in Babylon there was great unrest and war taking place around Israel. But now a time of rest had come across the region, so that Israel could return to the Promised Land, and the temple could be rebuilt.

By the time we reach Zechariah 6:8, we discover that the chariots going towards the North Country had given the Holy Spirit rest in the land of the north. So important is the work of the Holy Spirit in the plans of God that spiritual warfare takes place to give room for the Holy Spirit to work in the nations. This is why spiritual warfare is so important. Without spiritual warfare, the work of God can be held up for quite some time, as was the case with the rebuilding of the temple at Jerusalem.

Today, God wants you full of the Holy Spirit, equipped with the armor of God, and ready to do warfare in heavenly places; are you ready?

Reading: Zechariah Chapter 6

What Are You Waiting For?

Being filled with the Holy Spirit does not mean that you become so heavenly minded that you are no earthly good. The people of Bethel sent men to entreat the priests and the prophets at the house of the Lord, whether they should fast on the fifth month as they had always done (Zechariah 7:1-3). The word of the Lord came to Zechariah, where God asked the people if they had fasted these last seventy years for him or for themselves.

The point was that God was not looking for the people to get involved with a religious fast when the widowers, the fatherless, the foreigners or the poor needed help. They had become hard-hearted and covered their ears to the needs of those around them. God became angry with these people, because they did not listen to the laws or the words which the Lord had sent by the Holy Spirit through the earlier prophets.

Obedience is better than sacrifice or religion. And if there is enough evidence in both the Old Testament and the New Testament that we need the Holy Spirit, then what are we waiting for? Today, don't serve God through religious observance; serve God through obedience to the Holy Spirit!

Reading: Zechariah Chapter 7

Day 51

New Beginnings

In the first chapter of the first book of the New Testament, we find that Mary was found to be pregnant through the Holy Spirit (Matthew 1:-8). Remember what I said at the beginning of this book. The Holy Spirit is known as the *'Spirit of the Lord'* in the Old Testament, but he is known as the *'Holy Spirit'* in the New Testament; but they are one and the same person.

The operation of the Holy Spirit in the life of Mary indicates to us that God, through the Holy Spirit, brings new life by way of Jesus into the world at large. The birth of Jesus also brings new hope and a new way into the presence of God by his death at the end of his life. All this is accomplished because God the Holy Spirit was active at the start of Christ's life, and at the start of his ministry on earth.

If the Holy Spirit was active at the start of our conversion to Christ, then we need to ask ourselves, *"Is the Holy Spirit active at the start of our own ministries today?"* If the Holy Spirit is not active at the start of our own ministries, then we need to ask ourselves, who is? And if we are not sure, then it's time to seek God for the Holy Spirit!

Reading: Matthew Chapter 1

Day 52

Have You Got The Fire?

John the Baptist clearly taught that he baptized with water for repentance, but one would come after him and baptize people with the Holy Spirit and fire (Matthew 3:11). When I was a young Christian, it was easy to spot people around me who were on fire for God. In fact, being on fire for God was part of the language of Christianity for that era.

Sadly, in some parts of the modern church today, that term has disappeared. It is not easy to discover who's on fire for God in some churches, simply because people do not wait on God for the baptism of the Holy Spirit, as was the case many years ago. At one time, waiting for God to baptize people in the Holy Spirit would set young Christians on fire for God. And this is something that is needed in our churches today.

Serving God without the fire of the Holy Spirit within a person is hard work. That is because we have to rely on the flesh and our agendas to get the work done. There's nothing wrong with having an agenda. However, if we have an agenda without the fire of the Holy Spirit in our lives, then we have nothing. Ask God to give you the fire of the Holy Spirit today!

Reading: Matthew Chapter 3

Tuesday
7/19

Day 53

Are You In The Wilderness?

We discover, at the end of Matthew Chapter 3, that not only was Jesus baptized in water, but he was also baptized in the Holy Spirit. And if the baptism of the Holy Spirit was good enough for Jesus, then the baptism of the Holy Spirit is good enough for us too. Then, in Matthew 4:1, we discover that Jesus was led by the Holy Spirit into the wilderness to be tempted (or tested) by the devil.

Today, I hear about many Christians who go through difficult circumstances, wondering why they are having such a hard time. It is difficult to tell such people that God has allowed them to go through hard times so that the Holy Spirit can refine them through the fire of trials. If a wilderness experience was good enough for Jesus, it's good enough for us too.

Wilderness experiences allow God to put us through circumstances that will shake out the dross from our lives. We should not pray that God would take us out of the wilderness, but we should pray that God would give us the grace to go through it for the glory of God. If you are going through the wilderness experience today, don't resist, just trust God!

Reading: Matthew Chapter 4

Wed
7/20

Day 54

Who Are You Relying On?

The Pharisees could not understand by what power Jesus drove out demons in Matthew Chapter 12. They thought that he was driving out demons through the power of the devil. They could not distinguish that the things of God are accomplished by the power of the Holy Spirit. In other words, the Pharisees could not discern the difference between good and evil, even though they claimed to have a good understanding of the law.

Jesus could have said that he drove out devils through his own power, but he didn't. He involved and acknowledged the power and working of the Holy Spirit in and through his own life. He demonstrated that he needed to rely on the Holy Spirit and not upon himself, even though he was God the Son (Matthew 12:28).

If Jesus needed to rely on the Holy Spirit to get the job done, then so do we. And if we are not relying on the Holy Spirit to serve God, then who are we relying on? The church needs to get involved with the Holy Spirit more than at any other time in history. Today, will you acknowledge that you too need to rely on the Holy Spirit just like Jesus did?

Reading: Matthew Chapter 12

Day 55

Don't Blaspheme the Holy Spirit!

Not only did Jesus acknowledge his own need of the Holy Spirit in his ministry, he also warned the Pharisees not to attribute his miracles to the power of the devil in Mark Chapter 3. Jesus warned the Pharisees that people can be forgiven for all kinds of sin, but they cannot be forgiven for blasphemy against the Holy Spirit (Mark 3:28-29).

The reason that Jesus targeted the Pharisees about this issue of blaspheming the Holy Spirit was because they had become overly religious. They justified themselves by keeping the law, and not by following the leading of the Holy Spirit. Today, this is the danger for Christians who become overly religious, particularly when they advocate the doctrines of a particular denomination.

The more we promote a denomination or a particular religious viewpoint, the less we rely on the Holy Spirit. There is nothing wrong with belonging to a denomination, as long as that denomination does not become bigger than God. Today, if you are depending more on your church than the Holy Spirit, then it's time to focus yourself back on God.

Reading: Mark Chapter 3

58

Day 56

Don't Forbid Prophecy!

The ability to prophecy did not just come when the Holy Spirit was poured out upon the church in Acts Chapter 2. Prophecy was part of the Old Testament, as well as part of the Gospels and the New Testament. In Luke 1:67 Zechariah, the father of John the Baptist, was filled with the Holy Spirit and prophesied. He prophesied about the coming of the Lord and that his son John would prepare the way for Jesus (Luke 1:76).

Prophecy is one of the hallmarks of the work of the Holy Spirit in the life of a church. However, when people forbid the use of prophecy in a church or fellowship, then they are holding back the very thing that God would encourage. Such nay sayers usually come up with some kind of excuse for not permitting prophecy in churches today.) They will tell us that God does not work that way, or that prophecy might offend people or that we might expose ourselves to false prophecy.

In other words, any excuse is offered up to prevent God from moving through someone's life; through the power of the Holy Spirit. If you are in a church that does not permit the moving of the Holy Spirit, then get out now!

Reading: Luke Chapter 1

59

Day 57

After The Wilderness

On Day 53 we talked about Jesus being led into the wilderness. We also discussed the fact that God sometimes allows Christians to go through a wilderness experience to refine them. But the good thing about going through the wilderness is the fact that the same God who allows such an experience also brings us out of the wilderness in his time.

It says in Luke 4:14-15 that when Jesus came out of the wilderness, he returned to Galilee in the power of the Spirit. He began preaching in the synagogues, and everyone praised him. In other words, when we permit God to complete his refining work in our lives, then we become candidates for God to use us in powerful ways.

Even though you may have been going through a tough time lately, do not resist what God is trying to accomplish in your life. Not only does God justify us through the blood of the Lamb, he also glorifies us through the power of the Holy Spirit. Jesus has set us the example about how God wants to deal with each and every one of us. So let God complete the work that he has already started in you!

Reading: Luke Chapter 4

Day 58

Worship Through The Spirit

One of the exciting aspects of being filled with the Holy Spirit is our capacity to worship God in a way that we could never do in the flesh. No matter how we worship God, he is still pleased with us. However, when we learn to let God fill us with the Holy Spirit, then our worship will take on a new meaning for us.

When the seventy-two returned from a field trip preaching the gospel and casting out devils, in Luke 10:17-21, they returned to the Lord full of joy. Jesus warned the seventy-two not to rejoice that the demons were subject to them, but to rejoice because their names were written down in heaven. Jesus was so full of joy through the Holy Spirit that he worshiped God for revealing deep spiritual things to the unlearned.

Today, ask God to reveal to you how to worship him full of the Holy Spirit. Don't try and work up worship in the flesh, but allow God's Holy Spirit to have his way in your life, and learn to soar on wings like eagle. Then you will touch God's throne room like never before. Then you will know what it is like to really worship God in Spirit and in truth.

Reading: Luke Chapter 10

7/23

Day 59

Don't Turn Jesus Away!

One of the reasons why people will not ask to be filled with the Holy Spirit is because they are afraid that God will give them something that will take over their lives in the wrong sense. When we seek God in prayer, he will never give us something that will harm us. This is why Jesus said, in Luke 11:11-13, that if a son asks his father for a fish he will not be given a snake instead, etc.

Jesus went on to say that if someone who is evil knows how to give good gifts, then how much more will your Father in heaven give the Holy Spirit to those who ask him. And if Jesus is offering us the Holy Spirit when we ask for him, why do some people insist that we don't need the Holy Spirit today? Such a viewpoint contradicts the very words of Jesus.

The reason why some people don't accept the baptism of the Holy Spirit today is because they only know how to twist scripture to suit their own denominational standpoint. Today, Jesus is still offering to fill you with the Holy Spirit. So don't turn him away! Don't twist what scripture says about the Holy Spirit, just listen to the words of Jesus and respond to him!

Reading: Luke Chapter 11

Day 60

Are You Born Again?

Anyone who is truly born again has no problem with being filled with the Holy Spirit. This is because any true conversion to Christ involved the process of regeneration through the power of God the Holy Spirit. This is why Jesus told Nicodemus that no one can enter the kingdom of God unless they are born of both water and the Spirit (John 3:5).

We have raised a number of reasons in this book why people reject the workings of God the Holy Spirit in their lives. One further reason that some people reject the Holy Spirit is because they are not truly born again. Therefore, because they have not been regenerated, they cannot understand spiritual matters. This is why Jesus said in John 3:12 that if people could not understand earthly things, then they will not understand heavenly things?

When a Christian questions the work of the Holy Spirit in the lives of other believers, then we need to question whether they are truly born again. The flesh does not like the Holy Spirit, and religious folk don't like the term _'Born Again'._ Today, make sure that you are truly born again, and ready to be filled with God the Holy Spirit.

True

Reading: John Chapter 3

7/26

63

Day 61

God Is Not In A Building

When Jesus met the woman of Samaria, in John Chapter 4, they had a discussion about where was the best place to worship God; the mountain in Samaria or Jerusalem. But Jesus concluded his discussion about where the best place to worship God was. He stated that the best place to worship God was in Spirit and in truth (John 4:23).

Many times I have heard people ask the question, "Which is the best church to worship God in? Is it the Methodist Church, or the Baptist Church, or the Presbyterian Church or the Pentecostal Church?" The answer is that the best place to worship God is in our hearts, where the Holy Spirit resides. As much as people would like to, God cannot be contained in a box that relates to any one religious denomination.

I can attend any church I like. However, if God is not on the inside of me, then all that I have is empty religion. Just because I stand in a garage does not make me an automobile. Today, God still resides in people and not in buildings. And if your church is full of people who do not have the Holy Spirit on the inside of them, then you have nothing.

Wed

Reading: John Chapter 4

64

Day 62

The Flesh Counts For Nothing

I can be the busiest person in a church, but if what I do does not come through the inspiration of the Holy Spirit, then all that I have done is gratify my flesh. Jesus said in John 6:63 that the Spirit gives life but the flesh counts for nothing. Real life comes by the power of the Holy Spirit through God's word.

There is nothing worse than listening to someone preach the word, who has not been inspired by the Holy Spirit. I have witnessed people who are very articulate in putting sermons together, but when they preach there is no life in their words. We cannot effectively preach God's word if the life of the Holy Spirit is not at work within our own lives. When that happens all that we end up with is flesh.

Revelation from God's word is better than looking through any commentary to help us explain the bible. The bible without the unction and operation of the Holy Spirit does not work. The Holy Spirit is the key to unlocking the mysteries of God's word. So stop trying to do things in the flesh, and start trusting the Holy Spirit to lead you into God's word!

Then

Reading: John Chapter 6

7 / 28

¶ Day 63

Let The Holy Spirit Flow Through You

Many bible scholars believe that the Holy Spirit was present with God's people in the Old Testament, but that he would be in us in the New Testament. In John 7:37-39, Jesus said that anyone who believes in him, out of his inner most being would flow rivers of living water. Here Jesus was referring to the Holy Spirit, who would be given after he had ascended to heaven in Acts Chapter 1.

The best part of my Christian life, after being born again, is knowing that the Holy Spirit is flowing through me. I like nothing better than experiencing the anointing of the Holy Spirit upon me during the day. And I do not have to do anything to enjoy God's anointing flowing through me. All that I initially did was to invite the Holy Spirit to reside deep within me, when I originally got baptized with the Holy Spirit.

Today, I cannot imagine what life would be like without the Holy Spirit flowing through me like living water. And yet, many Christians purposely choose to live without the knowledge or the function of the Holy Spirit in their lives; do not let yourself become one of them!

Fri

Reading: John Chapter 7

7/29   66

Day 64

Has Someone Kept You From The Holy Spirit?

In John 14:15-17 Jesus told the disciples that if they kept the commandments, he would petition the Father to give them an advocate, who would be with them forever. The world cannot receive the Holy Spirit until they are first born again. But what is worse is when Christians do not receive the Holy Spirit, after they have been converted.

You may wonder why some Christians do not receive the Holy Spirit. Often the answer is because they have never been taught how to seek God until they are baptized in the Holy Spirit. (Some denominations teach that such an experience belongs to the Pentecostal and Charismatic Christians only.) The truth is that many denominations want to hold their congregations in bondage and away from the truth. The Holy Spirit is for everyone, and not just for one or two particular denominations.

Has someone in your church kept you from the Holy Spirit? Has someone told you that the Holy Spirit was only for the apostles? It's time to wake up and recognized that you have been lied to. The whole of scripture is for you edification, and today you need to seek out the Holy Spirit.

Sat

Reading: John Chapter 14

Day 65

Let The Holy Spirit Testify About Jesus!

When people deny the Holy Spirit they deny Jesus. Jesus said, in John 15:26, that when he sends us the Holy Spirit he will testify about him. The work of the Holy Spirit through us is to shine a light in the world, testifying about Jesus. And this testimony is not always about what we might say to people concerning Jesus. When the Holy Spirit is within us others will know that we have something, or someone, that they do not have.

Before I was born again, I knew that my Christian friend had something inside of him that I did not have. My friend never preached to me in words, but his life spoke volumes to me. He did not hide his Christianity, but he did not preach to me, not once. And yet, the Holy Spirit within him convinced me that I needed to become a Christian.

The Holy Spirit can take a lot of work out of trying to win the lost. When we ask the Holy Spirit to come inside of us, he will operate in ways that we know nothing about. He can touch people deep within their souls, in places we cannot reach by self-effort alone. Today, start asking the Holy Spirit to work through you, so that you can testify to others about Jesus!

Steph

Reading: John Chapter 15

7/31

Day 66

Let The Holy Spirit Speak To You!

The work of the Holy Spirit is multifunctional. It is impossible to recount in this book all that the Holy Spirit can do for us. In John 16:13-15 Jesus stated the Holy Spirit will lead us into all truth, he will tell us what is yet to come and he will receive revelation from Jesus and make it known to us. In other words, the Holy Spirit delights in doing all the work, rather than us trying to achieve something after the flesh, or through human endeavors.

Obviously the kingdom of God requires a certain amount of hard work; just ask anyone who is in full-time ministry. However, if we rely solely on our own efforts rather than on the Holy Spirit, then we make the anointing of the Holy Spirit redundant in our lives. As we read above, not only does the Holy Spirit guide us into all truth, he will reveal what is yet to come.

Learning to trust the Holy Spirit takes time, it is not something that will just happen overnight. What is required of us is to trust the Holy Spirit, believe in him and accept that he wants to communicate with us. If you have not been receptive to what the Holy Spirit is trying to say to you, then start today by allowing him to speak to you!

Reading: John Chapter 16

Day 67

Breathe On Me Breath Of God

One of the first things that Jesus did to the disciples, after he had risen from the dead, was to breathe on them so that they would receive the Holy Spirit (John 20:22). This he did so that the disciples would have the strength to carry on his work after he had ascended. Jesus gave the disciples many instructions about what to do after his death, part of which we will consider in Acts Chapter 2, in the next chapter of this book.

Although we have alluded to the experience of both being born again and the baptism of the Holy Spirit, we have not considered the source of these two different experiences. Jesus brings us the born again experience, through his death on the Cross, and makes us acceptable before God. However, the Holy Spirit comes directly as a promise from the Father, which is why only born again Christians can receive the baptism of the Holy Spirit.

This does not mean that non-Christians cannot feel God's presence; they just cannot receive the full baptism of the Holy Spirit until after they are converted. If Jesus saw the need to get his own disciples filled with the Holy Spirit, we should make sure that others do too.

Reading: John Chapter 20

Day 68

Wait For The Holy Spirit!

After the resurrection, Jesus and the disciples had two different agendas. The disciples wanted to know when Jesus was going to restore the kingdom to Israel. However, Jesus was more interested in getting his disciples baptized in the Holy Spirit (Acts 1:4-8). Jesus told the disciples that they would receive power once the Holy Spirit had come upon them. He told the disciples that they needed to wait in Jerusalem until they had been filled with the Holy Spirit.

Jesus did not tell the disciples to start going out and witnessing about him. He told them that they first needed to wait upon God so that he could baptize them in the Holy Spirit. It was in fact the Holy Spirit who would give them power to be witnesses. Too many people today attempt to go out witnessing without first waiting on God to receive the Holy Spirit; then they wonder why they become so weary in well-doing.

Have you ever spent time waiting on God to either fill you with the Holy Spirit, or refresh you with more of the Holy Spirit? If not, then today you need to start waiting on God to fill you with the power of the Holy Spirit!

Reading: Acts Chapter 1

Wed
8/3

71

Day 69

The Holy Spirit is For Everyone Who Comes To Jesus

When the disciples obeyed the instructions of Jesus and waited for the outpouring of the Holy Spirit on their lives, in Acts Chapter 2, they all were filled with the Holy Spirit and spoke in other tongues (Acts 2:4). Peter then preached to everyone, who had gathered to see what all the fuss was about. The crowds were convicted by what Peter had to say to them; and then they asked him what they should do (Acts 2:37).

Peter told the crowds that they needed to repent, be baptized and receive the gift of the Holy Spirit (Acts 2:38). But what was interesting about Peter's sermon was what he said to them next. He told them that the promise (of the Holy Spirit) was for all whom the Lord would call (Acts 2:39). Notice that! The Holy Spirit was not just for the apostles and followers at that particular time in history. He was for anyone who God called into his kingdom, including you and me.

If anyone tells you that the Holy Spirit is not for today, they are deceiving you. The Holy Spirit and his gifts did not die out with the apostles. So ask God to give you the Holy Spirit and see what happens next!

Reading: Acts Chapter 2

Thu
8/4

Day 70

Don't Test The Holy Spirit!

Because the Holy Spirit is part of the Trinity, he is able to act in judgment on those who would attempt to deceive him, or grieve him in some way. In Acts Chapter 5, Ananias and his wife Sapphira both lied to the Holy Spirit concerning how much money they brought to the apostles, after selling a piece of property (Acts 5:1-11).

Both Ananias and Sapphira were judged by the Holy Spirit and died for their deceit. In other words, God the Holy Spirit dealt with them in the same way that God the Father would have dealt with them. God the Father, God the Son and God the Holy Spirit are all one and in total agreement with each another. We cannot get around God by going to the Son or the Holy Spirit, hoping that they will act any different to each other; they are all in total unity.

You may ask why do we not see more people being judged in such a manner today. This is because God is merciful, and at the start of the church he had to let everyone know who was boss. But this does not mean that we should test the Holy Spirit. And those who test the Holy Spirit by stating that we don't need him in the 21st Century better beware!

Reading: Acts Chapter 5

Day 71

Choose Wisely!

The need for the power of the Holy Spirit in our lives is not limited to those who have dynamic ministries; like the people we may have seen on our Christian TV channels. We all need the Holy Spirit to help is in our daily lives, and each morning we need to ask God to lead us by the Holy Spirit; again, this we should do every day.

In Acts Chapter 6, the disciples were so busy preparing the word that some of the widows were being overlooked when it came to the distribution of food. To solve this problem, the Twelve asked everyone to select seven men full of the Holy Spirit and wisdom (Acts 6:3). This they did, and everyone was happy.

What criteria should we use just to appoint people who may wait on tables in our churches? Should we choose those who are experienced in waiting on tables, or those who are popular? No, we should choose those who are full of the Holy Spirit and wisdom. No matter what role a person operates within a church, musician, pastor or elder, all must be full of the Holy Spirit and wisdom, otherwise we are asking for trouble!

Reading: Acts Chapter 6

Sat
8/6

Day 72

Stand By The Holy Spirit!

There will always be a battle between those who are filled with the Holy Spirit and those who are religious. We only need to look at Stephen, who was brought before the Sanhedrin for performing great signs and wonders among the people in Acts 6:8. In Acts 7:51, Stephen did not pull any punches when he told the Sanhedrin that they were a stiff-necked people, who always resisted the Holy Spirit.

Stephen was martyred for standing by the Holy Spirit, who was working in his life to save and heal those who listened to him. He did not back down for one moment, and paid the ultimate price for his loyalty to God and the Holy Spirit. You may not be martyred for standing up for the Holy Spirit, but you may be asked to leave a church that does not operate in the gifts.

So important is the work of the Holy Spirit in our lives that we should never compromise our beliefs to satisfy the religious. Persecution often comes from the religious in churches, and not just from those who are non-believers. But when we are prepared to stand by the Holy Spirit, he will stand by us.

Reading: Acts Chapter 7

Sun
8/7

Day 73

Lay Hands On People!

When the apostles heard that people in Samaria had accepted the word of God, they sent Peter and John to them. When Peter and John arrived at Samaria, they discovered that the people had only been baptized in the name of Jesus. So they laid hands on them so that they might receive the Holy Spirit (Acts 8:15-17).

People who tell us that we only need to be baptized after receiving Christ have obviously not read this passage of scripture in Acts Chapter 8. People who state that we only need to be baptized in water are deceivers. Being born again is all that we need to become Christians, but if we want to live effective Christian lives, and then we need to be filled with the Holy Spirit.

God provides some people the faith to lay hands on other Christians, so that they might be filled with the Holy Spirit. So important is this ministry of laying on of hands that the apostles sent Peter and John to Samaria to perform this function. If you want to see people filled with the Holy Spirit, ask God to start sending you to those who are seeking after him and, by faith, start to lay hands on those who want more!

Reading: Acts Chapter 8

mon

8/8

Day 74

Start Speaking In Tongues!

(During the early period of the Book of Acts,) we can be mistaken for thinking that the Holy Spirit was only poured out on the Jews. We only need to turn our attention to Acts Chapter 10 to discover that the prayers of the Gentile, Cornelius, had reached the throne of God in heaven.

(God set about a chain of events, where he sent the apostle Peter to preach to the house of Cornelius about the death and resurrection of Jesus. Peter spoke about the events that took place in and around Galilee; including the work of the Holy Spirit through Jesus. While Peter was still speaking, the Holy Spirit was poured out on the house of Cornelius. The Jews who had come with Peter were astonished when they heard the house of Cornelius speaking in tongues and praising God.

I know churches where the believers would be shocked if they heard people speaking in tongues and praising God. However, this was not the case for Peter and his friends when they heard the house of Cornelius doing such a thing. As Peter stated in Acts Chapter 3, the Holy Spirit is for all those who are called into God's kingdom. So today, start speaking in tongues!

Reading: Acts Chapter 10

Tue
8/9

Day 75

Go With The Holy Spirit!

At the church in Antioch we find Barnabas, Simeon and Saul, who were prophets and teachers. While they were worshiping and fasting, the Holy Spirit told them to set apart Saul and Barnabas for the work which God had called them to do. Hands were laid on them and they were sent on their way (Acts 13:1-3). We presume that the Holy Spirit spoke to them through prophecy or the word of knowledge.

What is interesting about this passage of scripture is that God allowed Luke, who wrote the Book of Acts, to record the fact that people were instructed directly by the Holy Spirit. I am aware that some commentators suggest that the Holy Spirit only spoke to them because the bible had not yet been written; but this is nonsense.

I have personally experienced the Holy Spirit directly speaking to me and guiding me all through my Christian life, and he has never made a mistake. I want to encourage you today to let God the Holy Spirit direct your life and make decisions for you. Some people do not like the idea of letting the Holy Spirit take control of their lives, don't you be one of them!

Reading: Acts Chapter 13

Wed
5/10

Day 76

Do As God Pleases!

Learning to be led by the Holy Spirit also means knowing what we should and should not do as Christians, and where we should and should not go. Paul and his companions travelled around Phrygia and Galatia, but they were kept by the Holy Spirit from preaching the word in Asia (Acts 16:6). Notice that Paul and his companions only preached the gospel where the Holy Spirit led them.

Like you, I have met Christians who think that God has given them a license to do just as they please. To be quite honest, many of them follow the inclinations of their flesh without really being subject to God the Holy Spirit. They end up riding rough shod over other people's feelings, with no regard for the consequences of their actions.

Learning to be led by the Holy Spirit also means being willing to comply with the constraints that he puts on us. If we do not receive peace about doing certain things or going to certain places, then learn to let God's peace through the Holy Spirit guard your heart. Remember, the kingdom is about doing what the Holy Spirit pleases and not what we please.

Reading: Acts Chapter 16

Thu

8/11

79

Day 77

Take The Rough With The Smooth!

As we intimated in the last chapter, following the Holy Spirit does not mean that we do as we please and then hope that God approves. Following the Holy Spirit often requires us to die to self, and follow God's plan for our lives. We know that when Jesus was in the garden of Gethsemane, he had to put his own will down, so that he could take up God's will and die on the Cross for each and every one of us.

Paul was no different. He was compelled by the Holy Spirit to go to Jerusalem, knowing that prison and hardship awaited him (Acts 20:22-23). Paul did not pick and choose what he did or where he went for God. He took the good with the bad and the rough with the smooth, even when this meant that his life was at risk.

If we think that the kingdom of God is always going to be glamorous, then we are going to end up disappointed. If we think that everything will always be lined up so that we will always have a good time, and then we will never really develop spiritually as Christians. Learn to take the rough with the smooth, and like Paul, learn to walk by faith and not by sight.

Reading: Acts Chapter 20

Jue

8/1 2

Day 78

Don't Follow A Religious Code!

Today, there are still too many people who come to Christ and then end up following a religious code, often perpetrated through churches. They start off in the Spirit, but end up justifying themselves in the flesh. Justification only comes through Jesus and not through the rules of religious people.

In Romans 2:29 Paul said that circumcision of the heart takes place by the Holy Spirit and not by a written code. And yet today churches still hold their congregations in bondage, or under their control, by implementing their own religious doctrinal code that diverts people away from the real truth found in God's word. But why do some Christians still insist on following a religious code, rather than following the Holy Spirit?

The answer to that question can be found at the end of Romans 2:29. That is, some Christians look for justification and praise from other people and not from God. Today, do not let religious Christians influence you to justify yourself through the observation of a religious code or a denominational doctrine. Stay clear of such matters and keep trusting the Holy Spirit to guide you into all truth!

Reading: Romans Chapter 2

Day 79

Receive God's Love Today!

You may have come across people who state that the fruits of the Holy Spirit are more important than the gifts. Let me tell you something! When we receive the Holy Spirit we get both the fruits and the gifts, simply because (God does not separate the fruits from the gifts) God never gives us half the Holy Spirit; he gives us all of him.

(In Romans 5:3-5) Paul said that we could glory in our sufferings, because they produce perseverance in us. Perseverance produces character and character produces hope. Paul then said that hope will not put us to shame because God's love has been poured out into our hearts by the Holy Spirit.

(There are two specific types of love in the world.) We can possess human love in our hearts, and we can obtain God's love in our hearts by the Holy Spirit. There is nothing wrong with human love, but it is not the same as God's love. So, if you want to experience God's love in your heart today, then all that you need to do is open yourself up to the Holy Spirit, and God's love will be manifest through you.

Reading: Romans Chapter 5

Sun
8/14

Day 80

He Shall Quicken Your Mortal Bodies

(Not only do we receive eternal life when we are born again,) but we also receive spiritual life to help us on our earthly journey, before we reach heaven. In Romans 8:11 Paul said that if the same Spirit who raised Christ from the dead dwell in you then he will quicken your mortal bodies; and this is because the Holy Spirit dwells within us.

The Holy Spirit does not just provide us with direction, gifts and fruits, but he is also able to keep our mortal bodies going, especially as we get older. I once spoke to an elderly Spirit-filled Christian gentleman, and I asked him how old he felt on the inside. He told me that he felt like he was just a teenager. And the reason for this was because of the Holy Spirit that resided within him.

Although we age on the outside, Christians do not age on the inside. We do not age on the inside because we have a deposit of eternity within us, which does not age. The Holy Spirit within us is the deposit and guarantee of eternal life which is yet to come. So today, do not judge yourself by your outward earthly age, judge yourself from the inside!

Reading: *Romans 8:11*

Day 81

Joy In The Holy Spirit

It can take time for Christians to realize that the kingdom of God is not about rules and regulation, other than loving the Lord your God with all your heart, and your neighbor as yourself. In Romans 14:17 Paul said that the kingdom of God is not about eating and drinking, but righteous, peace and joy in the Holy Spirit.

The Holy Spirit makes known to us through scripture that Jesus has made us righteous, and that God has placed his peace within our hearts Because of this we have a joy which is unspeakable and full of glory. None of this can be manufactured in the flesh, through rules and regulations pertaining to the kingdom of God.

If you have to justify yourself before people rather than before God, and peace and joy is not your daily experience, then something has gone wrong somewhere. Today, if you want to enjoy a peace that passes understanding, then recognize that you need more of the Holy Spirit to accomplish such an attribute in your life. Even though Christianity can be a struggle, you should still have a peace within you blessing your day!

Reading: Romans Chapter 14

Tues

8/16

Day 82

Sanctified By The Holy Spirit

In Romans 15:16 Paul said that God raised him up to be a minister of Christ to the Gentiles, so that they might be an offering acceptable to God, sanctified by the Holy Spirit. Not only did Jesus shed his blood so that we would be cleansed from sin, his death also permitted the Holy Spirit to continue the work of sanctification in our lives.

Some Christians are put off by the word 'sanctification' because it smacks of rules and regulations; having to restrict ourselves in some way. However, when we recognize that it is by the Holy Spirit that we are able to put the deeds of the flesh to death, then it's not such a difficult word after all.

Sanctification is not something that always happens overnight. And people who struggle with addictions can often feel condemned because they have not been able to gain the mastery over their sins. However, when we ask the Holy Spirit to release us from the bondage of sin, we will start to see God doing a deeper work in our lives. But the work of the Holy Spirit in sanctifying us can take time. So today, do not panic if the work of sanctification is not complete in your life, it will be one day soon.

Reading: Romans Chapter 15

Wed
8/17

Day 83

Gifts Of The Holy Spirit And The Second Coming

As we have said before in this book, there are those who would suggest that the gifts of the Holy Spirit ended with the apostles. If that were the case, why would the apostle Paul say that we should not lack any spiritual gifts as we wait for Christ to be revealed; that is, at the Second Coming of Jesus (1 Corinthians 1:7)?

When Paul wrote this letter to the Corinthians, it was not intended as a private letter for their ears only. This letter was intended to eventually find its way into the bible to encourage those of us in the 21st Century. The closer we move towards the Second Coming of Jesus, the more we will need the gifts of the Holy Spirit to help us in our service for God.

Not only does God want you to watch for the Second Coming of Jesus, but he also wants you to be fully engaged in the kingdom of God. In order to be more effective in service for God, you need to be able to use all of the gifts of the Holy Spirit without fear or favor. Today, ask God to reveal to you the gift that the Holy Spirit has given to you. Then ask God to show you how to use them for the glory of the kingdom of God.

Reading: 1 Corinthians Chapter 1

86

Day 84

You Always Have A Safety Net

There are two ways of learning about the things of God. One way is to read the bible, and the other is to receive a revelation from the Holy Spirit; these ways are not mutually exclusive. In 1 Corinthians 2:13 Paul said that we do not speak in words taught by human wisdom, but we speak words by the Holy Spirit; explaining spiritual realities with spirit-taught words.

The bible helps us to stay on track and not go into error. However, that's only one part of the story. If we never venture into the area of the Holy Spirit because we are afraid that we might go into error, then we remain like a prisoner behind bars. God did not just give us the bible; he also gave us the Holy Spirit. I have seen people who are hot on the bible and still they end up in error.

The Bible is our safety net. However, if we never move out in the Holy Spirit, then we will never discover the fantastic revelations that God can give to us through him. And once you have received a revelation through the power of the Holy Spirit, you can always check back in with your safety net to see if it does not contradict God's word.

Reading: 1 Corinthians Chapter 2

87

Day 85

You Are The Temples Of The Holy Spirit

(God no longer lives in temples or churches today, as was the case in the Old Testament.) (In the New Testament, God moved his habitation away from temples and into human hearts.) This is why Paul says in 1 Corinthians 6:19-20 that our bodies are the temples of the Holy Spirit, who comes from God. In other words, we are no longer our own, we have been purchased through the blood of Jesus; therefore we should honor God with our bodies.

It is a sad state of affairs when God comes knocking on the door of a Christian's heart asking if s/he will receive the Holy Spirit, but the person locks the door. There are in fact two great sadnesses today. The first sadness is the person who will not let Jesus into their heart. The second sadness is the Christian who will not let the Holy Spirit into their lives.

I am grateful that God brought me into the knowledge of the Holy Spirit soon after I became a Christian. The Holy Spirit has been anointing me for over forty years, and he has never led me into error. Today, God wants people to stop fighting over the theology of the Holy Spirit and start experiencing his anointing.

Reading: 1 Corinthians Chapter 6

Day 86

Gifts Of The Holy Spirit

In 1 Corinthians Chapter 12 Paul did not want us to be ignorant concerning the gifts of the Holy Spirit. In 1 Corinthians 12:7-11 he listed the nine gifts of the Holy Spirit as the gifts of: wisdom; knowledge; faith; healing; miracles; prophecy; discerning of spirits; speaking in tongues; and interpretation of tongues.

How sad it must be for those who do not accept the gifts of the Holy Spirit in their churches today. Without these gifts of the Holy Spirit a vast amount of work in the kingdom of God would never be accomplished. If we had to rely on our own wisdom, our own knowledge, our own faith and to be blind to the deceptive spirits that would try to infiltrate our churches, then we are going to have a difficult time living for God.

No wonder so many churches end up in a mess, all because they think that they can survive by utilizing that which comes from the flesh. I have heard people say that they would never move in the gifts of the Holy Spirit because their church has always done things in a certain way. Today is the day when we need to start doing things God's way!

Reading: 1 Corinthians Chapter 12

Sun

8/21

Day 87

Will You Be God's Prophet?

In 1 Corinthians 14:1, Paul said that following on from love we should seek after the gifts of the Holy Spirit, particularly prophecy. Paul talks about the need for love in 1 Corinthians Chapter 13; a chapter neatly placed between the chapter on gifts and the chapter on prophecy. Some Christians use Paul's chapter on love as an excuse not to use the gifts of the Holy Spirit, but that's not what Paul was saying.

Paul was showing us that the gifts of the Holy Spirit work with the fruits of the Spirit and love; something that we have discussed in an earlier chapter of this book. When love is our motivation, then people have no right to question the use of the gifts of the Holy Spirit in our lives.

As we have also discussed in this book, God is looking for people who are prepared to become prophets, and bring God's word by the Holy Spirit to their churches. We use the bible to teach and encourage people, and we prophecy to give people inspiration and direction for their lives. Today, consider whether or not God is calling you to be one of his prophets. Do not seek the will of people on this matter, seek the will of God!

Reading: 1 Corinthians Chapter 14

Do Not Reject God's Deposit!

People make a big fuss about not getting involved with the Holy Spirit, and yet he is still only a deposit of better things to come. And this is exactly what Paul said in 2 Corinthians 1:22, that God has set his seal of ownership on us and put the Holy Spirit in our hearts as a deposit. When we resist the Holy Spirit we resist God, and we resist the better things to come in eternity.

Resisting, or rejecting the Holy Spirit and his gifts, is like a child refusing to accept presents from his or her parents. The Holy Spirit is proof of God's ownership over our lives. Some people do not recognize that rejecting the gifts of the Holy Spirit is actually a rejection of God. However, there comes a point when God will not always strive with those who constantly reject the work of the Holy Spirit in their lives and in our churches today.

Today we have so much to rejoice over, particularly the fact that God has guaranteed our salvation and eternal life by giving us the deposit of the Holy Spirit. The Holy Spirit is God, he is life and he is our all and all. Blessed are those who accept God's deposit of greater things to come.

Reading: 2 Corinthians Chapter 1

Tue
8/23

91

Day 89

The Law Or The Holy Spirit?

Some Christians get caught between starting out in the Holy Spirit and then ending up going back to the law. Paul addressed this problem in Galatians 3:3 & 3:5. Paul gets quite hot under the collar when he writes to the Galatians, who he knew started out in the Spirit, and then ended up going back to the law.

Paul asked the Galatians, did God give them the Holy Spirit and performed miracles among them through the law, or because they believed what they heard? When I first attended a church, I was told that I should come to Jesus just as I was. After I came to Jesus, the leaders of the church tried to put me in bondage by heaping rules and regulations upon me.

Thankfully I found myself another church, which concentrated on moving in the Holy Spirit, and I began to grow very quickly. Jealousy and control is often at the root of why people want to bind Christian in religion. Religion is not Christianity and Christianity is not religion. Today's word for the body of Christ is, do not to let the religious take control of the body of Christ and its members. God abhors such a thing!

Reading: Galatians Chapter 3

Wed
8/ 24

Day 90

Have You Got Your Full Armor On?

In Ephesians 6:13-18 Paul instructs us to put the full armor of God on. The problem for some folk is that they only manage to put on part of the armor. They put on the helmet of salvation, the breastplate of righteousness, the belt of truth, with their feet shod with the gospel of peace, which is fine and dandy. However, there's a bit more to the armor than that.

The armor also includes the shield of faith to extinguish the fiery darts of the evil one; and the sword of the Spirit, which is the word of God. However, there is one more thing. We need to pray in the Holy Spirit (tongues) on all occasions, and with all kinds of prayers and requests. We can have the armor on as tightly as we want, but if we do not pray in tongues, we are wasting our time.

God's armor is not just designed as a defense mechanism. God never intended that we should only defend ourselves. He expects us to engage in spiritual warfare, which can only be done when we pray in tongues. If you are used to only putting on your armor, maybe it's time to start waging spiritual warfare by praying in tongues.

Reading: Ephesians Chapter 6

Thru
8/25

Day 91

Unity In The Spirit

There is one thing that the Holy Spirit can do that no human institutions can do, and that is to bring unity to the body of Christ. In Philippians 1:27, Paul said that he knew the church would stand firm together in one Spirit. In fact, in Ephesians 4:4 Paul told us that there was one body and one Spirit and one hope, etc.

The Holy Spirit is a great unifier for those who receive Jesus into their hearts. The reason for this is that only those who are truly born again can be filled with the Holy Spirit. Therefore, when were filled with the Holy Spirit we are connected and unified with the rest of the body. Although wheat and tares grow together in the church, there are no tares that can be filled with the Holy Spirit.

Not only do individuals need to be filled with the Holy Spirit, whole churches need to be filled with him too. When churches make it part of their agenda to get their members filled with the Holy Spirit, then the tares will be less of a problem. Remember, tares don't want to be filled with the Holy Spirit; they only want to cause trouble.

Reading: Philippians Chapter 1

94

Day 92

Worship Through The Holy Spirit

When a church adopts the practice of getting people filled with the Holy Spirit, worship takes on a whole new meaning. In Colossians 3:16 we are encouraged to be filled with the Spirit speaking to ourselves in psalms and hymns and spiritual songs. In other words, once we have been filled with the Holy Spirit, we can enter a realm of worship that is simply not possible in the flesh.

God accepts all forms of worship from his people, whether they are filled with the Holy Spirit or not. However, those who are filled with the Holy Spirit can soar in the spirit like no one else. For one thing, those who are filled with the Holy Spirit can sing in the spirit and worship in unknown tongues, which is the language of angels.

But the most important aspect of worshiping in the Spirit is that breakthrough comes much easier than trying to gain such a breakthrough by self-effort alone. Remember, worship is a form of submitting and yielding to God, which brings us closer to God's throne room. Today, let the Holy Spirit bring you closer to God's throne as you worship him in Spirit and in truth!

Reading: Colossians Chapter 3

Sat

8/2 7

95

Day 93

Do Not Quench The Holy Spirit

There is a very short passage in 1 Thessalonians 5:19, which simply says that we should not quench the Holy Spirit. There is a balance between running a church according to our own agendas and letting the Holy Spirit have his way among us. Sadly, for many churches, the balance is tilted far too much towards the control of individuals rather than to the Holy Spirit.

The Holy Spirit cannot be disregarded or put in a box at the whim of someone's opinion. Because the Holy Spirit is a gentleman, he will not force himself on anyone. He waits for us to surrender more to God's will, so that he can have his way in our lives. And one of the best ways to see the Holy Spirit work more in our lives is when we surrender ourselves to God.

Submitting to God places us more in the hands of the Holy Spirit than anything else. In other words, we quench the Holy Spirit because we refuse to submit to God's ways. God and the Holy Spirit are in agreement with each other, just as Jesus and the Father are in agreement with each other. So if you don't want to quench the Holy Spirit, submit to God each day and see what the Holy Spirit will do for you!

Reading: 1 Thessalonians Chapter 5

Sua

4/28

Day 94

Do Not Fear!

I am still surprised by how many Christians come across as fearful. To be honest, I once went through circumstances that made me fearful. However, as I sought God, the Holy Spirit began to direct me in this matter. Each day, God showed me that I had to learn not to be fearful. This took a few weeks, but eventually God dealt with the fear in my life, and things improved dramatically for me.

In 2 Timothy 1:7 it says that the Holy Spirit, who God gave us, does not make us fearful. The Holy Spirit he gave us fills us with love, power and a sound mind. I would not have been able to get a handle on fear in my life if the Holy Spirit did not reside within me. And the more I have submitted to God, the more fear has been dealt with.

As we considered in the last chapter, and as we approach the end of this book, the biggest key to moving in the Holy Spirit is submission to God. A lack of humility in our lives suggests that we think that we can sort out our own lives. Remember, when we learn to submit to God, and then we become candidates for more of the Holy Spirit in our lives.

Reading: 2 Timothy Chapter 1

mon
8/29

Day 95

God Is A God Of Order

God does not do things our way, he does things His way. And when we learn to accept this, then things will go better for those who struggle with the things of God. In Titus 3:5, scripture tells us that God saved us because of his mercy, he saved us through rebirth and renewal by the Holy Spirit. As I have stated before, we only need to be born again to enter the kingdom of God.

The thief on the Cross had no time to get baptized or filled with the Holy Spirit. However, most of us do have time to enjoy all that God has got planned for us. And when scripture tells us that we are saved through new birth and receive renewal by the Holy Spirit, then we need to recognize that God the Father, God the Son and God the Holy Spirit all want to be involved in our lives.

There is a real need for a renewal of the Holy Spirit among the members of our churches. Many such people have become overburdened and worn down by the cares of this world. Today, the Holy Spirit can provide the renewal that people need, as they submit to God's order of things. Remember, doing things God way is one of the keys to His kingdom!

Reading: Titus Chapter 3

Tues

8/30

Day 96

The Holy Spirit Testifies To Our Salvation

The gifts of the Holy Spirit are a testimony to the great salvation that God has given to us. In Hebrews 2:3-4 scripture states that our salvation was first announced by the Lord and confirmed by those who heard him. Not only so, but God testified to this salvation through signs and wonders and gifts of the Holy Spirit, given to us according to God's will.

The gifts of the Holy Spirit and our salvation are actually all part of the same package. When we deny the Holy Spirit, we deny the very salvation that God has given to us. People who deny the gifts of the Holy Spirit are either not born again or very deceived. How sad it is for those who have denied the Holy Spirit all of their Christian lives.

Do not let yourself be influenced by those who are opposed to the Holy Spirit and his gifts, they are not doing you any favors. Today, if you are not fully persuaded about the need for the gifts of the Holy Spirit in your life, then search scripture and see what God alone has to say about the subject. And be warned, those who say that we can have the Holy Spirit without any of his gifts are also deluded.

Reading: Hebrews Chapter 2

Weel
8/31

Day 97

The Holy Spirit And Obedience

The work of the Holy Spirit in our lives is to sanctify us and make us obedient to God, as we have already discussed in this book. It says in 1 Peter 1:3 that we have been chosen by God through the sanctifying work of the Holy Spirit, so that we might obey Jesus Christ. And this is precisely why some people don't like the Holy Spirit; they are simply demonstrating their disobedience to God.

The problem with such people is that, if we are not too careful, such disobedience to God in other people can spill over into our lives. And then, not only are such people disobedient to God, they make us just as disobedient to him too. Theology only provides us with the theory of Christianity and not the practical experience of it.

Examine yourself today and determine for yourself whether or not your Christianity is theoretical, or it is full of the power of the Holy Spirit. Recognize that obedience to the Holy Spirit is obedience to God. Dismissing the Holy Spirit and his gifts is also disobedience to God. Today, decide whether or not you just want the theory of God's kingdom or you also want the power!

Reading: 1 Peter Chapter 1

Thur
9/1

Day 98

Don't Miss Out On The Holy Spirit!

We know that we live in Christ because we keep God's commandments (loving God and loving our neighbor as ourselves). In 1 John 3:24 the apostle said we will know that God lives in us by the Spirit he gave us. If we deny the Holy Spirit, then how can we know that God lives in us? The answer to that question is that we would need to guess that God lives in us if we continue to deny the Holy Spirit.

The Holy Spirit is the one who brings the reality of God's life within us to our attention. I have no idea how I would cope as a Christian today without the Holy Spirit. I have become so accustomed to his presence in my life that I would become very lonely without him. And for those who still doubt the Holy Spirit and his gifts today, there is one question that needs answering.

Why are there so many people across the world who testifies to being filled with the Holy Spirit? They cannot all be possibly wrong, and they cannot all be deluded. Today, you need to make certain that you are not missing out on the Holy Spirit. You also need to make sure that you are operating in the gifts that he has made available for you to use.

Reading: 1 John Chapter 3

Day 99

Do Not Be Deceived By The Doubters!

God has given us two important things to do in our Christian lives. One is to build ourselves up in the most holy faith and the other is to pray in the Holy Spirit (which is to pray in tongues), according to Jude 1:20. In Jude 1:21 we are told to do this until we are brought to eternal life. But how can we pray in the Holy Spirit if we don't fully accept his workings in our lives?

I will tell you how those who do not believe in the Holy Spirit and his gifts do this. They cut out any scriptures that mention the gifts of the Holy Spirit. To my astonishment I have literally seen people, who do not believe in the gifts of the Holy Spirit, do this when they preach. If that is not deception and false teaching at work, then I don't know what is.

It is my prayer today that you will not permit a living soul to continue to cast doubt on the work of the Holy Spirit in your life. I have had to cut people out of my life, who do not accept the workings of the gifts of the Holy Spirit in the lives of Christians today. I don't even bother to argue with them. I trust God and I have always trusted what his word alone has to say about the Holy Spirit. Today, my prayer is that you will do the same thing.

Read: Jude Chapter 1

Sat
9/3

Day 100

Prayer For The Holy Spirit

It is my hope and prayer that you have learnt a lot from this study on the workings of the Holy Spirit in the lives of the believer. I pray that you have started to recognize the presence and importance of the Holy Spirit, both in the Old Testament and in the New Testament. I also hope that this study has removed any doubt from your mind concerning how much each and every one of us needs the Holy Spirit and his gifts to function properly in the kingdom of God.

I would like to end this study by joining in prayer with you that God will fill you to overflowing with the power and anointing of the Holy Spirit. So please repeat the following prayer after me, and let God do an exceptional work in your life in the days to come.

Heavenly Father,

I submit myself to you right now in the mighty name of Jesus. I acknowledge that I am a Christian and I no longer doubt the work of the Holy Spirit and his gifts in my life any more. I ask you to fill me to overflowing with the Holy Spirit right now, in Jesus name, Amen!

Sun
9/4

Made in the USA
San Bernardino, CA
01 March 2016